I Wonder Why

Stars Twinkle

and Other Questions About Space

Carole Stott

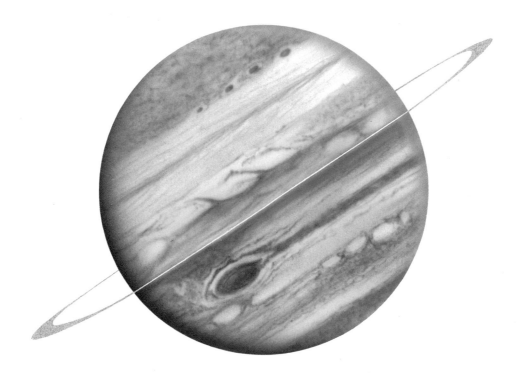

KINGFISHER

NEW YORK

KINGFISHER
Larousse Kingfisher Chambers Inc.
95 Madison Avenue
New York, New York 10016

First American edition in hardcover, 1993
First American edition in paperback, 1997
(HC) 10 9 8 7 6
(PB) 10 9 8 7 6 5 4 3 2

LIBRARY OF CONGRESS CATALOGING-IN-PUBLICATION DATA
Stott, Carole.
    Stars twinkle and other questions about space/
[author, Carole Stott].—1st Amer. ed.
        p. cm.—(I wonder why)
    Includes index.
    Summary: Answers questions about space such as,
"Are stars star-shaped," "Which is the coldest planet,"
and "What is a black hole."
    1. Astronomy—Miscellanea—Juvenile literature.
2. Space sciences—Miscellanea—Juvenile literature.
[1. Astronomy. 2. Outer space. 3. Questions and
answers.] I. Title   II. Title: Stars twinkle   III. Series.
QB46.S952 1993
520—dc20 92-44259 CIP AC

ISBN 1-85697-881-8 (HC)
ISBN 0-7534-5046-1 (PB)
Printed in Italy

Series editor: Jackie Gaff
Series designer: David West Children's Books
Author: Carole Stott
Consultants: Dr. David Hughes, Reader in Astronomy,
    Sheffield University
Art editor: Christina Fraser
Cover Illustrations: Chris Forsey, cartoons by Tony
    Kenyon (B.L. Kearley Ltd)
Illustrations: Chris Forsey, pp. 4-5, 31; Tony Kenyon
    (B.L. Kearley) all cartoons; Sebastian Quigley
    (Linden Artists) pp. 6-15, 18-21, 28-9; Ian Thompson
    pp. 16-17, 22-5; Ross Watton (Garden Studio) pp. 26-7;
    figure artwork on p. 19 Ruby Green.

FOR OWEN

CONTENTS

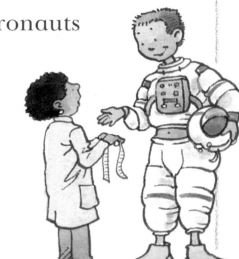

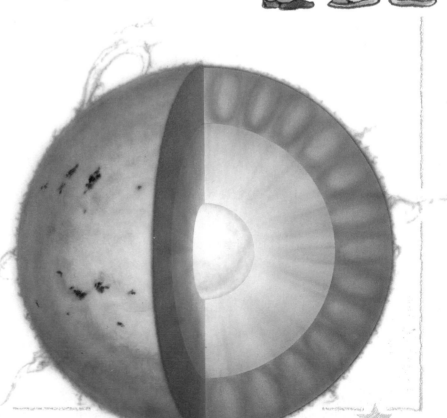

What is the universe?

The whole world and everything beyond it is the universe. It is all the stars and planets, the Earth and its plants and animals, you and me — everything.

● You are made of the same stuff as a star!

● There are huge groups of stars in space. They're called galaxies, and they're like gigantic star-cities.

● The Big Bang explosion sent the young universe flying out in all directions. Over vast ages of time, bits came together to make galaxies.

● The galaxies are still speeding apart today, and the universe is getting bigger.

When did it begin?

Many astronomers think that everything in the universe was once packed together in one small lump. Then, about 15 billion years ago, there was a gigantic explosion which they call the Big Bang.

● To see how the universe is getting bigger, watch the dots as you blow up a polka-dot balloon.

Will the universe ever end?

Some astronomers think the universe will just go on getting bigger as the galaxies speed apart. Others think that the galaxies may one day start falling back toward each other until they crash together in a Big Crunch!

● Astronomers are scientists who study the stars and the planets.

● No one knows where all the material to make the universe came from in the first place.

What is the Milky Way?

The Milky Way is the galaxy we live in. It is made up of all the stars you can see in the sky at night, and lots and lots more you can't see.

● The Milky Way is a spiral galaxy. Below you can see what it looks like from above — a bit like a whirlpool with long spiraling arms.

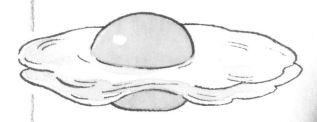

● From the side, a spiral galaxy looks like two fried eggs stuck together.

● The Milky Way got its name because at night we can sometimes see part of it looking like a band of milky white light across the sky.

● We live on a planet called Earth, which travels around a star called the Sun.

● Astronomers usually give galaxies numbers instead of names. Only a few have names that tell us what they look like — the Whirlpool, the Sombrero, and the Black Eye, for example!

● These are the three main galaxy shapes.

Irregular (no special shape)

Elliptical (egg-shaped)

Spiral

How many stars are there?

There are about 1,000 billion stars in the Milky Way. That's about 200 stars for every person living on Earth today!

Although we can't see all of it, astronomers have worked out how big the universe is and how many stars it has. There are about 100 million trillion stars, in around 100 billion galaxies. It's hard even to think about so many stars, let alone count them!

What are stars made of?

Stars aren't solid like the ground beneath your feet. Instead, they are made of gases like the air around you.

The two main gases in stars are called hydrogen and helium. They are the stars' fuel. Stars make heat and light from them.

● Sometimes huge flamelike sheets of glowing gas shoot out from a star. These are called prominences.

● Since earliest times, people have seen patterns in the way stars are grouped in the sky. The patterns are called constellations.

● The brightest star we can see in the night sky is called Sirius. Another name for it is the Dog Star. It is about twice as big as our Sun, but it gives out more than twenty times as much light!

Why do stars twinkle?

Stars only twinkle when we look at them from the Earth. Out in space their light shines steadily. We see them twinkling and shimmering because of the air around the Earth. As light from a star travels toward us, it is bent and wobbled by bubbles of hot and cold air.

Are stars star-shaped?

No, stars are round, like balls. We give them pointed edges when we draw them because this is what they look like from the Earth, with their light blinking and twinkling.

● Light bends when it passes through different things. If you put a straw in a glass of water, for example, it looks bent because it is half in air and half in water.

What is a red giant?

All stars are born, live for a very long time, and then die. A red giant is a huge old star.

● Stars are being born all the time. They start their lives in star-nurseries called clusters.

3 Most stars are like our Sun and shine steadily for nearly all their lives.

2 The gas and dust come together to make lots of balls, which become star clusters.

1 All stars are born in huge spinning clouds of gas and dust. Our Sun was born 4.6 billion years ago.

● If you think of our Sun as shining like a car's headlights, then a red giant would shine like a lighthouse!

4 Toward the end of their lives, stars like our Sun swell up and become as much as 100 times bigger. They turn into red giants. Our Sun will do this in about 5 billion years' time.

● On Earth, a sugar-lump-sized piece of a white dwarf would weigh as much as a small car!

5 When it has used up all its gas fuel, a red giant shrinks down into a white dwarf. It is then about 10,000 times smaller, but still very hot.

6 The star cools down and ends its life billions of years later, as a black dwarf — a cold black cinder.

● Stars must have at least eight times as much gas fuel as our Sun to end their lives in supernova explosions.

Which stars explode?

Different kinds of stars lead different lives. Some stars have a lot more gas fuel in them than others. These really massive stars don't die quietly, by cooling down. Instead, they blow up in a great flash of light. Stars that explode like this are called supernovas.

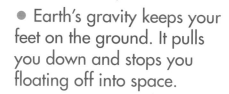

What is a black hole?

A black hole can happen when a massive star dies. The star falls in on itself, squashing all its material and becoming smaller and smaller. In the end all that's left is a place light cannot escape from — a black hole.

Everything in space has a pulling force called gravity — galaxies, stars, planets like the Earth, and even moons. Gravity holds things together and stops them floating off into space.

● Earth's gravity keeps your feet on the ground. It pulls you down and stops you floating off into space.

● When two large space bodies (like a planet and a moon) get close enough, there's a pulling contest between their forces of gravity. It's like a giant tug-of-war.

Stars that become black holes have really strong gravity — that's what pulls them inward and makes them collapse.

● A planet's gravity holds its moons to it and stops them shooting off into space.

● Light is sucked into black holes in much the same way as water is sucked down a bathtub drain.

● A star that gets too close to a black hole is sucked into it. Nothing, not even the star's light, can escape the pull of the black hole's gravity.

How hot is the Sun?

Like all stars, our Sun is a huge ball of superhot gas. It is hottest in the middle — the temperature there is around 27 million °F (15 million °C).

The outside of the Sun is a lot cooler than the middle — only 10,000 °F (6,000 °C). But this is still twenty times hotter than the hottest kitchen oven!

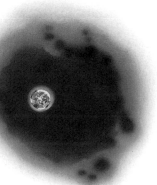

● Dark patches called sunspots come and go on the face of the Sun. They make it look as though it has chickenpox. Sunspots are dark because they are cooler and so give out less light than the rest of the Sun.

● Most sunspots are larger than the Earth.

● Plants and animals couldn't live without the Sun's heat and light.

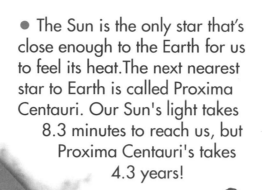

● The Sun is the only star that's close enough to the Earth for us to feel its heat. The next nearest star to Earth is called Proxima Centauri. Our Sun's light takes 8.3 minutes to reach us, but Proxima Centauri's takes 4.3 years!

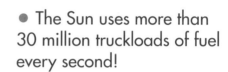

● The Sun uses more than 30 million truckloads of fuel every second!

Will the Sun ever go out?

One day the Sun will use up all its gas fuel and die. But this won't happen in your lifetime, or your children's, or even your great-great-great grandchildren's! Astronomers think that the Sun has enough gas fuel to last for at least another 5 billion years.

How many planets are there?

Our planet, the Earth, has eight neighbors. Together they make a family of nine planets which travel around the Sun. We call the Sun, and all the space bodies that whirl around it, the solar system.

Besides the Sun and the planets, the solar system includes moons, mini-planets called asteroids, and comets.

● The word planet comes from the Greek word *planetes*, which means "wanderer."

● Comets are a little like huge dirty snowballs. Most stay out on the edge of the solar system, but a few travel close to the Sun. These comets grow gas and dust tails, millions of miles long, when the Sun's heat starts to melt them.

Mars

Mercury   Venus   Earth   Jupiter

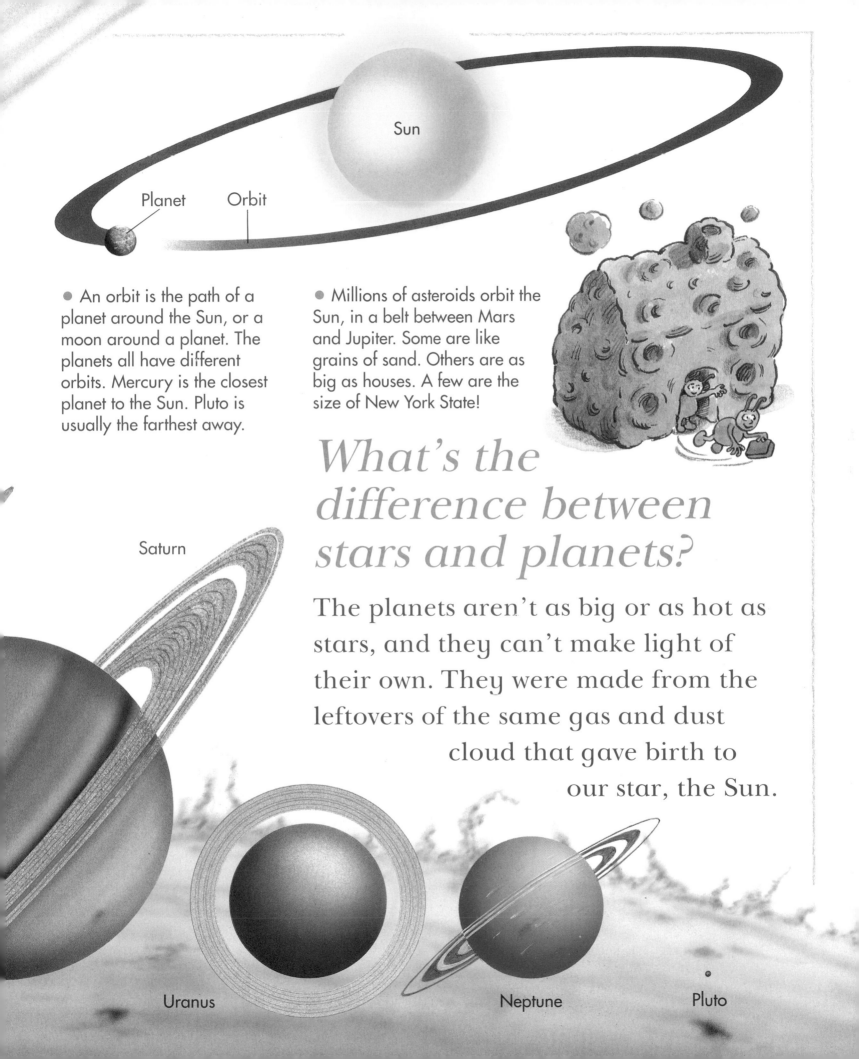

Sun

Planet   Orbit

• An orbit is the path of a planet around the Sun, or a moon around a planet. The planets all have different orbits. Mercury is the closest planet to the Sun. Pluto is usually the farthest away.

• Millions of asteroids orbit the Sun, in a belt between Mars and Jupiter. Some are like grains of sand. Others are as big as houses. A few are the size of New York State!

What's the difference between stars and planets?

The planets aren't as big or as hot as stars, and they can't make light of their own. They were made from the leftovers of the same gas and dust cloud that gave birth to our star, the Sun.

Saturn

Uranus

Neptune

Pluto

Why is Earth special?

Our planet is the only one in the solar system with water and living things on it. That makes it very special. It is the third planet from the Sun, and it gets just the right amount of heat and light to keep us alive. Any closer, and it would be too hot. Any farther away, and it would be too cold.

• When the Sun turns into a red giant star, it will swallow up Mercury and get so large that it will cover half of our midday sky.

• You can see what happens as the Earth spins if you turn a globe in the beam of light from a flashlight.

• All planets spin as they orbit the Sun.

Why does the Sun go out at night?

It gets dark at night because the Earth is spinning as it orbits the Sun. As parts of the Earth spin away from the Sun, they move out of its light into darkness. It takes a whole day and a night for the Earth to spin around once.

• Although astronomers think that millions of stars in the universe have families of planets, no other solar systems have yet been found.

Which is the hottest planet?

Venus isn't the closest planet to the Sun, but it is the hottest. The temperature there can reach 900 °F (500 °C) — that's about eight times hotter than it gets in the Sahara Desert, the hottest place on Earth.

● Although Mercury (right) is closer to the Sun, Venus is hotter! This is because Venus is covered by clouds of gas which act like a blanket, keeping in the Sun's heat.

● Space probes have landed on Venus and sent back pictures and information to Earth. The probes were destroyed soon after landing, however, by the terrible climate on Venus.

• Mars is the next planet after ours from the Sun, and people once thought that like the Earth it might have living things. Space probes were sent, but they didn't find any signs of life!

Which is the Red Planet?

• Mercury is covered in craters — hollows made by huge space rocks crashing into it.

• If you could visit Mercury, you would see that the Sun looks more than twice as big there as it does from Earth. This is because Mercury is so much closer to the Sun.

Mars is often called the Red Planet. The ground there is covered in dusty red soil, which gets swept up by the wind to make pink clouds! The rocks on Mars have lots of iron in them, and iron turns red when it rusts. A better name for Mars might be the rusty planet!

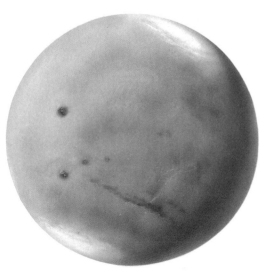

• Living things need water. If there is any on Mars, it is frozen inside its north and south polar ice caps.

Which is the biggest planet?

Jupiter is so huge that all the other planets could fit inside it! The beautiful patterns on its face are made by swirling clouds of gas, stirred up by powerful windstorms.

● Jupiter's Great Red Spot is so big that two Earths could fit inside it! It is a gigantic storm that has been raging for over 300 years.

● Jupiter was named by the ancient Romans, after the king of their gods.

● Jupiter is one of four planets with rings around them.

Great Red Spot

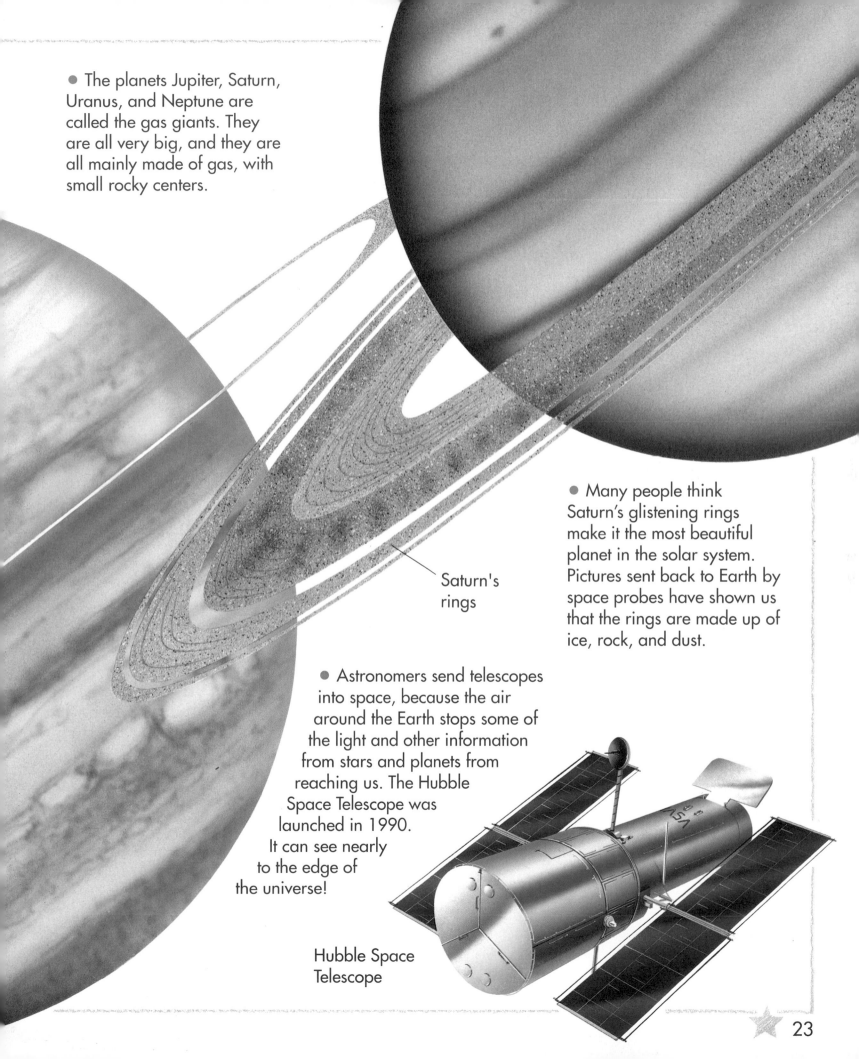

● The planets Jupiter, Saturn, Uranus, and Neptune are called the gas giants. They are all very big, and they are all mainly made of gas, with small rocky centers.

Saturn's rings

● Many people think Saturn's glistening rings make it the most beautiful planet in the solar system. Pictures sent back to Earth by space probes have shown us that the rings are made up of ice, rock, and dust.

● Astronomers send telescopes into space, because the air around the Earth stops some of the light and other information from stars and planets from reaching us. The Hubble Space Telescope was launched in 1990. It can see nearly to the edge of the universe!

Hubble Space Telescope

Which planet is farthest from the Sun?

Although for most of the time Pluto is the most distant planet, every 248 years its orbit brings it closer to the Sun than Neptune!

● Between 1979 and 1999, Pluto's orbit makes Neptune the farthest planet from the Sun.

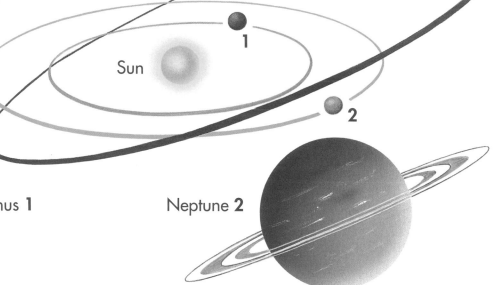

Pluto **3**

3

Sun

1

2

Uranus **1**

Neptune **2**

● One of the gases in Uranus is called methane. It gives the planet its blue-green color.

Which is the coldest planet?

Ice cream would taste as hot as soup on Pluto, where the temperature is an unbelievably icy -400 °F (-240 °C)! Pluto is so cold because it is very far from the Sun. It is almost 40 times farther away than the Earth is.

How do we know about the farthest planets?

Until the U.S. Voyager 2 space probe visited Uranus in 1986 and Neptune in 1989, not a lot was known about these two planets. They are too far away for us to see them clearly from Earth, even through the most powerful telescopes.

Voyager 2's cameras showed that Neptune has eight moons. Earth-based astronomers could only see two using telescopes.

● Voyager 2 left the Earth in 1977 and reached Neptune twelve years later, in 1989.

Which planet has the biggest moons?

Moons are rocky bodies that orbit planets. Jupiter has sixteen moons, and three of them — Ganymede, Callisto and Io — are larger than the Earth's Moon.

Mercury and Venus are the only planets that don't have moons. All the other planets have at least one.

Ganymede

Io

Our Moon

Callisto

● In pictures taken by the space probe Voyager 2, Io looks like a giant cheese and tomato pizza. The tomato color comes from volcanoes.

What is it like on our Moon?

The Earth's Moon is dry, dusty, and lifeless. There's no air to breathe or water to drink. During the day it's so hot that your blood would boil. At night it's freezing cold — not a good place to take a vacation!

UNITED STATES

Which planet's moons look like potatoes?

Mars has two tiny moons that look like lumpy old potatoes. They're called Deimos and Phobos and, unlike larger moons, they aren't round.

● On July 20, 1969, two American astronauts became the first living things ever to set foot on the Moon. Their names were Neil Armstrong and Buzz Aldrin, and their space mission was called Apollo 11.

● If the Earth were the size of an orange, then the Moon would be the size of a cherry.

● The Moon's gravity isn't as strong as the Earth's. You'd be much lighter on the Moon—only a sixth of your Earth-weight. So you'd be able to jump six times as high!

27

How fast do space rockets go?

Rockets have to go faster than 7 miles (11 km) per second to get into space. This works out to about 25,000 miles (40,000 km) per hour — and car drivers can get into trouble for speeding at 70 miles (110 km) per hour! If rockets didn't travel so fast they wouldn't be able to escape the enormously strong pull of the Earth's gravity.

Saturn V

- The tallest rocket ever launched was the Saturn V that took the Apollo 11 into space, and the first people to the Moon.

Space shuttle

Ariane 4

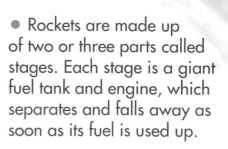

- Rockets are made up of two or three parts called stages. Each stage is a giant fuel tank and engine, which separates and falls away as soon as its fuel is used up.

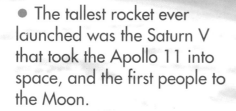

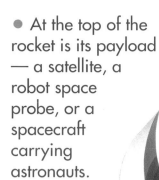

- At the top of the rocket is its payload — a satellite, a robot space probe, or a spacecraft carrying astronauts.

What are rockets used for?

Rockets are mainly used to put machines called satellites into orbit around the Earth. Different kinds of satellites are launched to do many different jobs.

- Satellites can be used by one country to spy on another.

- Satellite photographs and maps help scientists to study the Earth and what it's made of.

- Communications satellites pick up and send on TV and telephone signals.

- Navigation satellites help ships and aircraft to find their way.

- Some satellites help us to work out what the weather will be like.

Why do astronauts wear space suits?

There's no air to breathe in space and, depending on whether a spacecraft is in or out of the Sun's light, it's either very hot or very cold. Without space suits to protect them outside their spacecraft, astronauts would die.

● Astronauts have to wear seatbelts to stop them floating away when they use the toilet. Space toilets don't flush. Everything is sucked away instead.

● Astronauts sleep in bags that are strapped down to stop them floating around. Astronauts even have to tuck or tie their arms in to stop them waving around!

● Space stretches you — astronauts can come back as much as 2 inches (5 cm) taller!

Why do astronauts float in space?

Gravity is everywhere. But astronauts on board a spacecraft orbiting the Earth can't feel it or see it working. Out there, the Earth's gravity isn't strong enough to hold them down and they float around like balloons.

● The gold visors on their helmets protect the astronauts' eyes from the Sun's harmful rays.

● Backpacks called MMUs help astronauts to move around outside the spacecraft. They have oxygen for the astronauts to breathe, and a radio so that they can talk to people in the spacecraft and back on Earth.

Index